Advisory Committee on Dangerous Pathogens

INFECTION RISKS TO NEW AND EXPECTANT MOTHERS IN THE WORKPLACE

IN THE WORKPLACE

A guide for employers

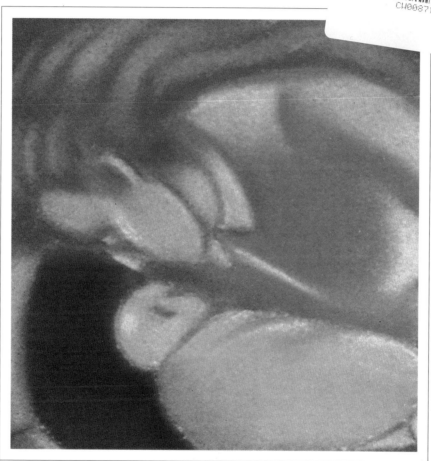

HSE BOOKS

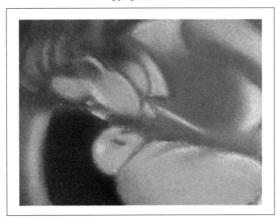

This guidance was prepared in consultation with HSE, by the Advisory
Committee on Dangerous Pathogens, which was appointed by the
Health and Safety Commission as part of its formal advisory structure
and by Health Ministers. The guidance represents what is considered
to be good practice by members of the Committee. It has been agreed
by the Commission and Health Ministers. Following the guidance is
not compulsory and you are free to take other action, but if you do
follow it you will normally be doing enough to comply with the law.
Health and safety inspectors seek to secure compliance with the law
and may refer to this guidance as illustrating good practice.

CONTENTS

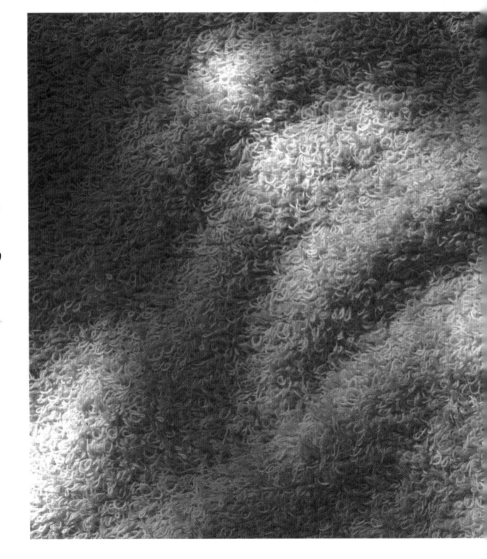

This publication is a guide for employers on protecting the health and safety of employees who are new or expectant mothers. It deals with the risk of infections in the workplace.

INTRODUCTION

1   Pregnancy is part of everyday life.

Being pregnant does not mean that you are

ill, but some infections, if they are

contracted in pregnancy, can affect the

health of the mother and baby. In very rare

cases, the baby may suffer serious harm and

this may result in permanent disability or

even death.

2   In most cases these infections are much more likely to be caught in the community (outside of work). But for some women there will be a risk at work. For example, they could be exposed to infection hazards in a microbiology laboratory, from contact with microbes (germs).

3   Health and safety law says that employers must assess the infection risks to all employees (male and female) when assessing risks from their work activities. The law also says that employers must do what is reasonably practicable to prevent or control the risks. They must pay particular attention to the risks which may affect new and expectant mothers.

4   The HSE publication *New and expectant mothers at work: a guide to employers*[1] gives general guidance on the law and on potential risks to pregnant and breastfeeding employees.

5   This publication is a guide for employers of women in jobs where there may be a risk of infection. It supplements the guidance on pages 18 and 19 of the general guidance and explains the nature of infection in pregnancy.

6   The emphasis in this guidance is that any infection risks which may affect pregnant employees can usually be controlled by normal risk management procedures required by, eg the Control of Substances Hazardous to Health Regulations 1994(COSHH)[2]. Many pregnant or breastfeeding women continue to work in jobs where there is a risk of infection and they and their babies come to no harm.

INFECTION

How people are infected

7   Infection occurs when a microbe (germ), such as a virus, bacterium, fungus or parasite, enters the body and multiplies. In some cases this can happen without any obvious symptoms.

8   Infection can occur through:

- the mouth, via contaminated fingers, or contaminated food or water;
- breathing in infected droplets in the air;
- splashes on to the eye or other mucous membrane such as the lining of the nose and mouth;
- broken skin when it comes into direct contact with an infectious microbe;
- injury by a sharp instrument such as a contaminated needle, or by the bite of an infected animal or insect;
- sexual intercourse.

9   Babies may also become infected from their mothers:

- in the womb (across the placenta);
- at the time of delivery (when the baby passes through the birth canal);
- from contaminated breast milk.

10   Each type of microbe usually has a specific way of entering the body. But in some cases infection can occur by more than one route.

The body's defence against infection

11   The intact skin and the lining of the mouth, throat, gut and airways provide a barrier to infection. The cells of these linings, and the substances that they produce, provide a first line of defence. If a microbe does cross this barrier, the body's next line of defence is the *immune system*.

12   Whether or not an infection occurs depends on a contest between the invading microbe and the body's immune system. This contest is partly responsible for the wide variety of signs and symptoms often seen during illness.

13   The way the body's immune system works is highly complex in detail, but can be easily understood in general terms. An important part of the immune system is the 'antibody response'. An invading microbe may stimulate the production of special proteins called antibodies. These latch on to the microbe and lead to its destruction and if the same type of microbe invades again, the body can quickly make new antibodies and prevent infection. The person is then considered to be *immune*, in other words, they can fight off the infection and do not get ill. This is the principle behind vaccination, where the body is exposed to all or part of the microbe in a controlled way. The immune system produces antibodies and in the future is able to resist the microbe when it attacks for real.

14   There are two ways of becoming immune to infection.

(a)   **Actively -** this is when a microbe enters the body and stimulates antibodies, or when someone is immunised with a vaccine. With some infections such as diphtheria, or whooping cough, immunity is virtually permanent. However with others, such as the common cold, immunity lasts only for a short time.

(b)   **Passively -** this is when a particular type of antibody is transferred to someone who does not already have it. This can take place when they are injected with concentrated antibodies made from someone else's blood. An unborn baby can also   acquire passive immunity when its mother's antibodies enter its bloodstream through the placenta. Likewise, antibodies can enter the baby in breast milk. Antibodies acquired passively only remain present and effective for a short time. For example, a mother's antibodies do not usually stay in her baby's bloodstream beyond 6-9 months of age.

15   Laboratory tests can be used to detect antibodies to show if a person is immune to a particular microbe, or not.

16   If the immune response cannot prevent an infection, the result of being infected can be:

Subclinical (inapparent) infection	Few if any outward signs or symptoms of the disease occur, but laboratory tests may show that infection has taken place.
Acute infection	Symptoms occur which range from mild to severe, usually with full recovery after a short period.
Persistent and latent infection	The microbe continues to multiply or may remain dormant within the person even though they are not ill any more. There may be no symptoms but the person may remain infectious for some considerable time, even for life. For example, some cases of hepatitis B infection can remain present but with no symptoms, also some microbes, particularly viruses, can remain hidden within the body's cells and this is called latent infection. These hidden microbes may be reactivated when some stimulus, such as stress, causes them to grow and produce symptoms. An example is 'shingles' which can occur many years after chickenpox.

INFECTIONS IN PREGNANCY

Are pregnant women at greater risk?

17   Usually, during pregnancy women are no more likely to catch an infection than at other times. In some cases, however, such as chickenpox, the infection may be more severe in pregnancy. But in most cases pregnant women will become ill in just the same way as other women.

18   It is important, however, to remember that if a mother does become infected, some infections may be dangerous for the baby.

What are the possible effects of infection on the baby?

19   The vast majority of infections in pregnancy have no effect on the baby. But the baby may be harmed by:

- some viruses, such as rubella (German measles);
- some bacteria, such as *Listeria*, and;
- some parasites, such as *Toxoplasma*.

20   If the baby is infected in the womb this could lead to:

- no signs or symptoms of disease;
- premature birth;
- acute infection or death before birth;
- birth defects, such as damage to nervous system and developmental problems;
- persistent infection;
- miscarriage.

Occupations at risk

21   Infections caught at work are rare. The level of risk will depend on the type of work and the control measures in use.

22   Examples of where infection hazards

may incur at work include those occupations where there may be contact with:

- human blood and body fluids such as genital secretions, which may be infected;
- infected animals including parrots, turkeys, pigeons, ducks, cats, rodents, rabbits and sheep (during lambing);
- laboratory cultures etc;
- water or food contaminated by human or animal faeces.

23   For details on some of the specific infections, see Appendix 2.

WHAT IS THE EMPLOYER'S REPONSIBILITY?

24   The purpose of the COSHH Regulations 1994[2] is to make sure that, as far as is reasonably practicable, you adopt adequate control measures which prevent or minimise risks to your employees from their work.

25   The COSHH Regulations state that you must assess all risks in the workplace. This includes, when appropriate, any risk of infection to your employees resulting from their work. You should produce a general assessment for all employees, including women of child-bearing age if they are part of the workforce. However, it may be necessary to adopt extra control measures, to ensure the health and safety of a particular worker and/or her child.

26   **An important point to remember is that you only need to act when the risk of infection arises from the work itself. Pregnant or breastfeeding mothers may well catch infections from other staff, just as they might from their friends and family outside the workplace. These infections are not the employer's responsibility under health and safety legislation.**

27   However, the one time you should consider the infection risk from other workers is when a pregnant woman is carrying out first-aid duties.

28   Employers should make the results of the assessment available to employees or their representatives. If women are present in the workforce, two types of risk assessment are required:

- a general assessment of risks which focuses on the three broad types of

hazard: physical, chemical and biological;

- a special assessment of risks to a particular employee when she tells you that she is pregnant or is breastfeeding.

29   You should consider the following factors when assessing the infection risks to any employee:

- the types of infection likely to be transmitted at the work;
- the possible sources of infection. For example, infected people and animals, their blood, body fluids and wastes, or contaminated environments and objects;
- the likelihood that a possible source of infection, eg a farm animal, is actually infected;
- the number of different sources of infection that staff may come into contact with and how often contact may occur;

- the control measures in use to protect employees;
- the medical history of the employee;
- the history of previous infection or immunisation;
- the need for suitable information, instruction and training for employees which will help them to prevent or reduce risk.

Action to be taken

30   The risk assessment needs to take into account if any female staff are of child-bearing age. For these staff, the assessment may show that there is a greater risk of infection at work than outside work. If it does, you should inform them about the risk and set up suitable control measures.

31   You should reassess the situation and if necessary take specific action if a woman employee declares in writing that she is pregnant, has given birth in the last six months, or is breastfeeding. An employer may ask her to produce a certificate from a registered medical practitioner, or a registered midwife, confirming her pregnancy.

32   Employers may find that it is impossible to deal with the increased risk to the woman. If this is the case, employers must consider adjusting her work, or offer alternative work or grant leave. Full details are in the general guidance[1].

Breastfeeding

33 Employers should make sure that staff who are breastfeeding are not exposed to risks that could damage their health or safety or that of their baby. There is no fixed timespan for breastfeeding and it can vary considerably. It is not uncommon to breastfeed babies for up to a year. Some mothers may continue for even longer.

34 Employers may wish to provide a safe environment in which female staff can express their breast milk and store it in a fridge. This is not, however, a legal requirement.

35 There is a danger that certain microbes (see Appendix 2) can be transmitted to the baby through the breast milk. This may result in an infection. However, this is unlikely in the workplace if adequate controls are in place (see paragraphs 40-48). This means that only on very rare occasions will you need to offer alternative work, or grant leave, to staff who are breastfeeding.

36 A more serious concern is where breastfeeding staff are working with chemicals that can enter the breast milk (eg lead or pharmaceutical drugs). Further advice on this is given in the general guidance on breastfeeding mothers[1].

What is the employee's reponsibility?

37   Employees also have a responsibility for their own safety. You should encourage them to take up offers of immunisations or health checks recommended, for example, by your occupational health advisor. Make it clear that they need to inform you as early as possible, in the event of pregnancy, or if they are breastfeeding. This will give you time to re-assess any risks and take any necessary action.

38   If there has been a delay in notifying you of the pregnancy, and your re-assessment shows an increased risk of infection, then you should tell the employee to seek further advice (see paragraphs 49-50).

39   You may also wish to remind pregnant employees of the general health advice that her GP or midwife will have given her about minimising the risk of catching infections from people in the wider community, including workmates.

CONTROL MEASURES

40 Most infection risks can usually be avoided or minimised by careful use of simple control measures. These include :

- preventing puncture wounds, cuts and abrasions, especially in the presence of blood and body fluids;
- avoiding the use of, or exposure to, sharp objects (needles, glass, metal, knives etc) where possible. If this is not possible, take particular care in their handling, cleaning and disposal;
- protecting all breaks in exposed skin by means of waterproof plasters and/or gloves;
- protecting the eyes and mouth with a visor or goggles/safety spectacles and a mask when there may be splashing;
- avoiding people or their clothing getting contaminated by using waterproof/water-resistant protective clothing, plastic apron etc;

- making sure staff wear rubber boots or plastic disposable overshoes when the floor or ground is likely to be contaminated;
- using good basic hygiene practices in the workplace, including hand-washing, and avoiding hand-to-mouth or hand-to-eye contact, smoking, eating, drinking, applying cosmetics or removing/inserting contact lenses, taking medicines etc;
- controlling surface contamination by containment and appropriate decontamination procedures;
- disposing of all contaminated waste safely.

41 Appendix 2 gives details of suitable control measures for some specific infections.

Immunisation

42 Safe working procedures are the first line of defence against infections at work. However, in some specific cases, the risk assessment may show that immunisation (vaccination) is necessary. For example, it may be needed for certain laboratory and health care workers. Immunisation should only be carried out under the direction of a medical practitioner. They will know when immunisation is not advisable. For example, there are some vaccines which should not be given to women while they are pregnant (see paragraphs 49-50). Immunisation should be seen only as a useful supplement to safe working procedures and the proper use of protective equipment and should not replace them.

43 Before an employee's pregnancy begins, it is in their interest and yours to make sure that vaccinations are available and used to provide protection against any infections. Make every effort to encourage this.

Information, instruction and training

44 If you carry out work that exposes any employees to a risk of infection you must provide them with suitable and sufficient information, instruction and training.

Information

45 You must tell your staff about:

- the health risks resulting from possible exposure;
- the precautions they should take.

Instruction

46 The purpose of instruction is to ensure that employees do not endanger themselves or others from exposure to anything that is infected.

47 You should tell staff clearly:

- the procedures for reporting their pregnancy;
- what cleaning, storage and disposal procedures are required, why they are required and when they are to be carried out;
- the procedures they must follow in an emergency;
- what they should do, what precautions they should take and when they should take them.

Training

48 Staff must be trained so that they understand and can use effectively the:

- methods of control;
- personal protective equipment; and
- emergency measures.

Where can I get advice?

49 Professional advice and publications on various aspects of infection in the workplace are available for you and your employees from a range of sources. These include:

- safety representatives;
- company or local occupational health departments;
- professional and trade associations;
- Employment Medical Advisory Service (EMAS), which is listed under the Health and Safety Executive in the telephone directory;
- trade unions.

50 For advice of a more general nature, other sources of information include:

- general practitioners (GPs);
- local consultants in communicable disease control or public health medicine in the Public Health Department at your local health authority;
- Health Boards;
- the Public Health Laboratory Service, and;
- the Departments of Health.

APPENDIX 1 RELEVANT LEGISLATION

Advice and further information on this legislation is available from the Health and Safety Executive, and in the references shown in Appendix 4.

Legislation

- Control of Substances Hazardous to Health Regulations 1994: Schedule 9 of these Regulations brought into force a European Directive on the control of biological agents and provided an approved list of biological agents.

- Management of Health and Safety at Work Regulations 1992: These cover a wide range of duties to do with worker protection.

- Management of Health and Safety at Work (Amendment) Regulations 1994: These brought into force a European Directive, aimed specifically at protecting women at work who are pregnant or breastfeeding.

- Employment Protection (Consolidation) Act 1978: This sets out an employee's entitlements to payment on maternity leave.

- The Workplace (Health, Safety and Welfare) Regulations 1992: These require suitable rest facilities to be provided for workers who are pregnant or breastfeeding.

- The Reporting of Injuries, Diseases and Dangerous Occurrences Regulations 1995: These Regulations require the notification of specified injuries, diseases and dangerous occurrences affecting people at work[3].

- Genetically Modified Organisms
  (Contained Use) (Amendment)
  Regulations 1996: These require risk
  assessment, and in some cases
  notification to HSE, of all activities
  involving the contained use of
  genetically modified organisms.

APPENDIX 2 INFECTIOUS MICROBES AND PREGNANCY

This section considers some of the infections that are known to present a risk to the fetus or new-born baby. Usually, there will be no greater chance of picking them up at work than at home or in the community. They are included here, however, to provide basic information for staff who might be concerned about them during pregnancy. Further information should be available from your occupational health advisor or from the other sources of information listed in paragraphs 49-50.

The list does not contain every type of infection. The infections are listed in alphabetical order.

Chlamydia psittaci

Organism: *Chlamydia psittaci* (there are several types and they have preferences for different animal hosts).

Sources: Infected birds, eg parrots (psittacosis), turkeys, pigeons and ducks (ornithosis), and sheep during lambing.

Disease in adults: Infections caught from birds are abrupt with fever, cough and often severe headache. This may lead to pneumonia. Infections caught from sheep may show no symptoms, or be a flu-like illness with headache, chills, fever, joint pains and dry cough and sometimes light-sensitivity, vomiting, and sore throat. Infection may be more severe in pregnancy, particularly after the third month. As well as the symptoms described above, the mother and baby may develop problems with kidney and liver function, and abnormal blood clotting. This severe disease is caught mainly from sheep. It can cause spontaneous abortion.

Duration: The incubation period varies between 5-21 days.

Effects on the unborn child: Infection from sheep may result in the death of the unborn child or premature delivery, which generally occurs 3-8 days after the symptoms first appear. If the pregnancy survives the acute infection, there appears to be no risk of long-term harm or birth defects.

Transmission to the baby: Across the placenta.

Likelihood: Transmission across the placenta to the baby can occur during serious infections. However, in pregnant women infection is often without obvious symptoms.

Examples of occupations at risk: Agricultural workers, farmers, pet shop workers, veterinary workers, etc.

Control measures: Avoid ewes, new-born lambs, and placentas at lambing time. Avoid clothing and boots that have been in contact with infected animals.

Risk statement: In England and Wales the PHLS Communicable Disease Surveillance Centre (CDSC) receives 0-9 reports of *C. psittaci* infection in pregnant women every year (3 cases were reported to CDSC during 1995, at least one of these was acquired at work).

Cytomegalovirus

Organism:	Human cytomegalovirus (CMV).
Sources:	Humans - particularly children. Transmission may occur through breast milk, saliva, sexual intercourse and blood.
Disease in adults:	Usually no symptoms in healthy people. It may cause an illness with symptoms similar to glandular fever (infectious mononucleosis).
Duration:	Acute illness in adults may last 2-3 weeks, then virus persists in a latent state.
Effects on the unborn child:	Usually no symptoms. A small number of babies may have symptoms at birth and can suffer long-term complications including damage to the nervous system, learning disability, and deafness.
Transmission to the baby:	Across the placenta.
Likelihood:	In the UK about three babies in every 1000 are born with this infection. But 90% of them have no symptoms. Some 5-10% of the babies who have no symptoms later develop CMV related problems. When infection takes place, damage can occur at any time during the pregnancy.
Examples of occupations at risk:	Those in close contact with children, eg nursery workers and health care workers, especially in children's wards.
Control measures:	Pay scrupulous attention to hygiene, including handwashing. Particular care should be taken when handling nappies, excreta etc from babies and children. No vaccine is available at present, but about 50% of women in the UK are immune because they caught the infection in early life.
Risk statement:	A virus of low infectivity. Transmission is easily prevented if you are aware of the hazard and set up simple hygiene measures.

Hepatitis A

Organism:	Hepatitis A.
Sources:	Humans, and water or food contaminated by faeces[*].
Disease in adults:	The severity of disease is closely related to age. Severe (fulminant) hepatitis is rare. In adolescents and adults symptoms are more severe and last longer than in children, who are often asymptomatic. Common symptoms and signs include fever, headache, jaundice, loss of appetite, nausea, vomiting and abdominal pain from a tender, enlarged liver.
Duration:	There is an incubation period of 15-45 days with a average of about 28 days. There is no risk of transmission one week after jaundice and darkening of the urine have appeared. There is no persistent or latent infection (carrier state).
Effects on the unborn child:	Mothers may transmit the infection to their unborn baby but it is very rare.
Transmission to the baby:	The virus multiplies mainly in the liver and passes into the faeces through the bile duct. Most transmission to babies is via mouth contact with faecally-contaminated objects (faecal-oral route).
Likelihood:	Mother to unborn baby transmission is very unlikely to occur.
Examples of occupations at risk:	Nursery workers, primary school workers, sewage workers, etc.
Control measures:	Pay scrupulous attention to hygiene, especially handwashing. A vaccine is available for adults and children but it is not currently licensed for use in babies under 1 year old.
Risk statement:	In developing countries people are usually infected in childhood and acquire lifelong immunity. In recent years in industrialised countries rates of infection have been variable and many children and adults are not immune. This is probably due to improved hygiene.

[*]Hepatitis E is transmitted in a similar way to hepatitis A and infections have been reported in the UK, but usually in travellers returning from abroad. The symptoms are similar to hepatitis A and there is also no persistent or latent infection (carrier state). However, there is a high death rate for pregnant women infected with the virus. There is no vaccine available.

Hepatitis B

Organism:	Hepatitis B.
Sources:	Humans, contaminated needles, blood and body fluids such as genital secretions[4] and laboratory specimens etc★.
Disease in adults:	Infection may cause acute inflammation of the liver (hepatitis) which may be life-threatening. A person showing no symptoms may still carry the infection (5% or less of adults have chronic infection). These people can develop severe chronic hepatitis, cirrhosis and primary liver cancer.
Duration:	The severity of the illness and the extent and duration of the jaundice can vary. A small proportion of patients develop severe (fulminant) hepatitis.
Effects on the unborn child:	Most babies infected at birth carry the infection, but show no obvious symptoms or the symptoms are mild and there is no apparent jaundice. Severe (fulminant) hepatitis in newborn babies has been reported but is very unusual.
Transmission to the baby:	The virus does not usually cross the placenta. It is thought that the mother passes the infection to her baby during delivery and just after by exposure to her blood.
Likelihood:	Risk of transmission from an hepatitis B infected mother to her baby may be as high as 90% depending on the stage of her infection. They will remain infectious and are at increased risk of developing chronic liver disease and liver cancer in later life. Hepatitis B antibodies and Hepatitis B vaccine given to a newborn immediately after birth is 85-95% effective in preventing them becoming carriers.
Examples of occupations at risk:	Health care workers, dentists, laboratory workers, rescue workers and other people exposed to human blood and body fluids.
Control measures:	Avoid injuries with sharp objects contaminated with blood and body fluids and direct contact with blood and body fluids. Use protective clothing. Ensure that all employees who might be at occupational risk are immunised and blood tests show them to be immune.

*Hepatitis C and D are transmitted in a similar way and require the same precautions. Immunity to hepatitis B will also protect people against hepatitis D, but no vaccine to hepatitis C is available. Hepatitis C infection from mother to baby has been reported but is uncommon.

Human immunodeficiency viruses

Organism: Human immunodeficiency virus (HIV) 1 and 2.

Sources: Humans, contaminated needles, blood and body fluids, laboratory specimens etc[4].

Disease in adults: Acquired immunodeficiency syndrome (AIDS) and related conditions.

Duration: Life-long, persistent infection.

Effects on the unborn child: Infection may lead to AIDS and other diseases.

Transmission to the baby: Across the placenta, during delivery and by breastfeeding.

Likelihood: The risk of transmission from an infected mother to baby (excluding breastfeeding) is 12-25%. Recent studies have shown that anti-viral therapy (azidothymidine AZT) given to HIV infected women during pregnancy, at delivery, and to their babies, will reduce the transmission rate.

Examples of occupations at risk: Health care workers, dentists, laboratory workers, rescue workers and other people exposed to human blood and body fluids.

Control measures: Avoid injuries with sharp objects contaminated with blood and body fluids and direct contact with blood and body fluids. Use protective clothing.

Risk statement: Infection at work is rare. The risk of transmission from an injury that pierces the skin involving known HIV positive blood is approximately 1 in 320 (0.3%). The risks can be reduced by awareness of the transmission route, adequate training, safe work practices and the use of simple control measures.

Listeria

Organism: *Listeria monocytogenes.*

Sources: Contaminated food (eg unpasteurised soft cheese, pâté, prepared salads such as coleslaw, and microwave-ready meals), infected animals, and silage.

Disease in adults: The symptoms of infection are like mild flu, but can have serious consequences for the unborn baby.

Duration: The incubation period varies between a few days to 10 weeks. How long the infection lasts also varies.

Effects on the unborn child: If septicaemia and meningitis occur in the baby the death rate is between 50-100%. The fetus may be aborted or born prematurely. There can be long-term effects in many organs including the airways, eyes and nervous system.

Transmission to the baby: Across the placenta, and during delivery.

Likelihood: Transmission can occur to the baby during severe infection in the mother. *Listeria* may also invade the mother's genital area and either infect the baby by travelling up into the womb (which is rare), or infect it during birth.

Examples of occupations at risk: Laboratory workers, food workers, farm workers, abattoir workers.

Control measures: Good laboratory practice - make sure staff avoid infection through the mouth. Good hand hygiene is very important.

Risk statement: Approximately 25 pregnant women catch *Listeria* each year in the UK. It is not known how many of these are caught at work.

Parvovirus

Organism: Human parvovirus B19.

Sources: Humans - via respiratory secretions.

Disease in adults: Parvovirus causes Fifth disease (erythema infectiosum or slapped cheek syndrome). About 50% of infections show no symptoms. The most common disease is a mild upset with fever in 15-30% and a characteristic rash. It can be confused with rubella. Joint problems are unusual in children, but common in adults, especially women.

Duration: The incubation period is usually 4-14 days, but may be as much as 20 days. Symptoms may continue for weeks and sometimes months.

Effects on the unborn child: Fetal death and spontaneous abortion may occur in the second and third trimesters. In some cases, this is associated with severe fluid accumulation (less than 10% of exposed fetuses).

Transmission to the baby: Across the placenta.

Likelihood: About a third of babies of infected women are infected in the womb.

Examples of occupations at risk: Health care workers, laboratory workers, teachers and child care workers.

Control measures: Basic good hygiene. Additional control measures may be needed where pregnant women are exposed at work to infected people in whom viral excretion may be prolonged because they do not have a fully working immune system or have certain other blood disorders.

Risk statement: It has been suggested that the increased risk of death of the unborn baby following parvovirus infection in pregnancy is around 9%.

Rubella

Organism:	Rubella virus.
Sources:	Humans by close contact and via respiratory secretions.
Disease in adults:	Usually mild and includes a faint reddish purple rash, sometimes accompanied by mildly inflamed eyes and joint pains.
Duration:	Acute illness lasts for less than 1 week in an adult.
Effects on the unborn child:	Many infected babies have no ill effects. However a wide range of birth defects including deafness, eye disease (cataracts), heart defects, an abnormally small undeveloped head (microcephaly) and learning disability can occur.
Transmission to the baby:	Across the placenta.
Likelihood:	Mass immunisation has reduced the risks of infection in pregnancy to a very low level. But if non-immune mothers catch rubella in the first 3 months of pregnancy, approximately 80% of the babies will have some rubella-associated problems. Between 12 and 16 weeks of pregnancy the risk of harm falls to about 5% and rarely occurs after that.
Examples of occupations at risk:	Laboratory workers, health care workers, especially in childrens' wards, nurseries etc.
Control measures:	Rubella vaccine is given routinely to all children, and adults who have not had the infection. Screening for immunity is routine in antenatal clinics, so that those that are not immune can be offered vaccination after that pregnancy.
Risk statement:	Women from overseas may not have been immunised against rubella and have the highest risk of any group of women in the UK. Between January 1991 and June 1994 in the UK 14 infected infants were reported. Nine of the 12 mothers were from overseas. In 1996 an unusually high incidence of rubella infection in Scottish men resulted in infections in 3 non-immune pregnant women.

Toxoplasma

Organism:	*Toxoplasma gondii.*
Sources:	Hand-to-mouth contact with the faeces of infected cats, contaminated soil, poorly washed garden produce, and by eating undercooked, infected meat (especially beef, lamb and pork).
Disease in adults:	Primary infection often has no symptoms. However, symptoms can vary from persistent acute fever with enlarged lymph glands to very rare infection in the brain, muscle and eye, leading to death. If people do not have a properly working immune system (immunosuppression) the dormant infection can return with serious consequences.
Duration:	Varies and may be lifelong.
Effects on the unborn child:	Most infected babies (90-95%) have no symptoms at birth, but some may develop eye damage in later life. Those with symptoms at birth may have accumulation of fluid in the brain (hydrocephalus), brain damage, inflammation of eyes and various non-specific signs.
Transmission to the baby:	Across the placenta.
Likelihood:	The overall risk of transmission from an infected mother to the unborn baby is about 40%. This ranges from about 15% in the first trimester to about 60% in the later stages of pregnancy. But the likelihood of an infected baby being harmed is much higher when infection occurs in early pregnancy than in later pregnancy.
Examples of occupations at risk:	Veterinary workers, cattery workers, farm/meat/abattoir workers, grounds maintenance staff, park keepers.
Control measures:	Avoid handling infected meat, cat faeces, and sheep at lambing time, or wear gloves and pay scrupulous attention to hygiene, including handwashing.
Risk statement:	In the UK, less than 20% of pregnant women are immune. A pregnant woman's immunity depends on their country of birth. People born in southern Europe or Africa are more likely to be immune. It is estimated that in the UK toxoplasmosis occurs in approximately 2 in every 1000 people, but most cases show no symptoms.

Varicella-zoster (chickenpox)

Organism:	Varicella-zoster virus (VZV).
Sources:	Humans by direct contact, droplet infection or recently soiled materials such as handkerchiefs.
Disease in adults:	Primary infection with VZV results in chickenpox. The severity varies but symptoms are generally more severe in adulthood. Following chickenpox the virus persists as a latent infection in the nervous system. It may return as shingles following reactivation of the virus.
Duration:	Acute illness usually lasting 2-3 weeks, after which the virus persists in a latent state.
Effects on the unborn child:	Skin scarring; brain damage with resultant learning disability; limb abnormalities.
Transmission to the baby:	Across the placenta.
Likelihood:	Infection in the baby is a rare complication of chickenpox in pregnancy. There is no evidence of risk to the baby if the mother has shingles.
Examples of occupations at risk:	Health care workers, nursery workers, school teachers.
Control measures:	Hospital occupational health departments may enquire routinely about chickenpox in staff and test those without a history for antibody to VZV. If women are not immune from past infection, contact with known cases of chickenpox or shingles present in the workplace should be avoided.
Risk statement:	Chickenpox may be more severe in pregnancy than in non-pregnant women. The risk of adverse effects in the unborn baby is highest in the second trimester (2% risk) and low in the first trimester (less than 0.5% risk). Newborn babies are at particular risk of severe chickenpox if infected from the mother in the first four days of life, although they can be protected with VZV antibodies (varicella-zoster immune globulin).

Other microbes

A wide range of microbes cause infections in the human population and may also infect pregnant women. They may or may not have an adverse effect on the baby. These include:

Borrelia burgdorferi (Lyme disease);

Coxiella burnetii (Q fever);

Campylobacter spp. and *Salmonella* spp (gastroenteritis);

Lymphocytic choriomeningitis virus (LCM),

Mycobacterium tuberculosis (TB),

Treponema pallidum (syphilis).

Any severe infection, whatever the cause, may be detrimental to the health of the mother and child. You should take this into account when you set up control measures to tackle the risks of infection in your workplace.

Members

Professor D J Jeffries (Chairman)
Department of Virology, St Bartholomew's
and Royal London School of Medicine and
Dentistry, London.

Mr K Ashley
Health and Safety Executive, Bootle.

Lt Colonel T Brookes (since April 1996)
MoD Chemical Defence Establishment,
Salisbury.

Professor G E Griffin
Division of Infectious Diseases, St George's
Hospital, London.

Mrs T McGuire
Director of Lothian NHS Occupational
Health Service, Edinburgh Health Care NHS
Trust, Edinburgh.

Colonel E Parry (until March 1996)
MoD Chemical Defence Establishment,
Salisbury.

Professor C Peckham
Institute of Child Health, London.

Ms H Tivey
MSF representative.

Dr T D Wyatt
Microbiology Department, Mater Hospital
Trust, Belfast.

Secretariat

Dr P J Gosling (Department of Health).

Mrs E Lawrence (Department of Health)
(from December 1995).

Ms A McGinty (Department of Health)
(until August 1995).

Dr M Bale (Health and Safety Executive).
(from September 1996).

Ms J Deans (Health and Safety Executive)

Mr P Lister (Health and Safety Executive)
(until August 1996).

APPENDIX 4 REFERENCES AND FURTHER READING

References

1   *New and expectant mothers at work: A guide for employers* 1994 HSE Books ISBN 0 7176 0826 3

2   *COSHH: The new brief guide for employers* IND(G)136L (revised) 1996 HSE free leaflet

3   *Everyone's guide to RIDDOR '95* HSE 31 1996 HSE free leaflet

4   *Protection against blood-borne infections in the workplace: HIV and hepatitis* 1995 Advisory Committee on Dangerous Pathogens HMSO ISBN 0 11 321953 9

Suggested further reading

Getting to grips with manual handling: a short guide for employers IND(G)143L 1993 HSE free leaflet

Remington J S and Klein J O *Infectious disease of the fetus and newborn infant*(4th edition) 1995 W B Saunders, Philadelphia

Rubella 1996 SODH/CMO(96)3 The Scottish Office Department of Health

Immunisation against infectious disease 1996 UK Health Departments HMSO ISBN 0 11 321815 X

Other publications of the Advisory Committee on Dangerous Pathogens

Precautions for work with human and animal transmissible spongiform encephalopathies 1994 HMSO ISBN 0 11 321805 2

BSE (Bovine Spongiform Encephalopathy): Background and General Occupational Guidance 1996 HSE Books ISBN 0 7176 1212 0

Microbiological risk assessment: An interim report 1996 HMSO ISBN 0 11 321990 3

Vaccination of laboratory workers handling vaccinia and related poxviruses infectious for humans 1990 HMSO ISBN 0 11 885450 X

Categorisation of biological agents according to hazard and categories of containment (4th edition) 1995 HSE Books ISBN 0 7176 1038 1

Guidance on the use, testing and maintenance of laboratory and animal flexible film isolators 1985 Available free of charge from the Health and Safety Executive, Health Directorate, Rose Court, 2 Southwark Bridge, London SE1 9HS

The priced publications are available directly from either:

The Stationery Office   or   HSE Books
The Publications Centre   PO Box 1999
PO Box 276   Sudbury
London SW8 5DT   Suffolk CO10 6FS
Telephone orders: 0171 873 9090   Tel: 01787 881165
General enquiries: 0171 873 0011   Fax: 01787 313995
Fax orders: 0171 873 8200

and through good booksellers.

INDEX

INFECTION RISKS to new and expectant mothers in the workplace *Questionnaire*

To help us assess this publication, will you please complete this questionnaire (tick box or ring number as appropriate) and return it to the address overleaf. Postage is free.

Name: ....

Company/organisation: ....

Address: ....

....

....

....

Post code: ....

Telephone number:...

Fax number:...

Nature of business:

Manufacturing

       Main activity: ....

Laboratory

Research

Warehousing

Professional services

Local/National government

Trade Association

Employees Association

Educational establishments

Did you find the guidance: *Very useful*   *Not useful*

                                           1   2   3   4

Was the information presented: *Well*   *Poorly*

                                           1   2   3   4

Was the layout: *Clear*   *Difficult to follow*

                                           1   2   3   4

Would you like to receive further information about other ACDP publications?   Yes ☐   No ☐

Did the publication contain the information you expected?   Yes ☐   No ☐

If not, what other information would you have expected?

....

....

....

Did you feel that the publication represents: *Very good value*   *Poor value for money*

                                               1   2   3   4

Have you taken any action or changed any procedures as a result of reading this publication?   Yes ☐   No ☐

If so, what?

....

....

Have you any other comments about this publication?

....

....

....

Thank you for taking the time to answer these questions

QUESTIONNAIRE

- - - - - - - - - - - THIRD FOLD - - - - - - - - - - -

FIRST FOLD

SECOND FOLD

```
┌─────────────────────────────┐
│ BUSINESS REPLY SERVICE      │
│ Licence No. LV 5189         │
└─────────────────────────────┘
```

Health and Safety Executive
Room 303
Daniel House
Stanley Precinct
Bootle
Merseyside L20 3QY

IR

- - - - - - - - - - - FOURTH FOLD - - - - - - - - - - -

Tuck A into B to form envelope
Please do not staple or glue

Printed and published by the Health and Safety Executive   7/97   C100